Also by Amin Khan

IN FRENCH:

*Colporteur*, Sned, 1980

*Les Mains de Fatma*, Sned, 1982

*Vision du Retour de Khadija à l'opium*, Isma, 1989

*Archipel Cobalt*, MLD, 2010

FORTHCOMING:

*Arabian blues*, MLD, 2012

# Amin Khan

# *Vision of the Return*

*Translated from the French by Dawn-Michelle Baude*

THE POST-APOLLO PRESS
Sausalito, California

Copyright © Galerie Isma, Algeria, 1989
Copyright © The Post-Apollo Press, 2012, U.S. edition
ISBN 978-0942996-75-3

LIBRARY OF CONGRESS CATALOGING-IN-PUBLICATION DATA
Khan, Amin, 1956-
  [Vision du retour de Khadija à l'opium. English]
  Vision of the return / Amin Khan ; translated from the French by Dawn-Michelle Baude.
    p. cm.
  ISBN 978-0-942996-75-3 (alk. paper)
  I. Baude, Dawn-Michelle, 1959- II. Title.
  PQ3989.2.K3885V5713 2011
  841'.92—dc23                    2011026977

Cover design and drawing by Simone Fattal
Book design and typeset by AEM Book Design in Granjon with Centaur display

The Post-Apollo Press
35 Marie Street
Sausalito, California 94965
www.postapollopress.com

# Contents

The Sleepy Telegraphist    *1*

Wild Donkey and Solitudes    *29*

Poems of Immobile Love    *45*

Vision of the Return of Khadija to Opium    *55*

# The Sleepy Telegraphist

Eyelids lowered
partial worlds
quiet

One soluble morning
I held
exhausted scents

and I believed
that life was
possible

Oblique sky
stars and vines
cries covered
with night's silence

the stairs rise and again descend
your throat
unmoving
drinks

sweet burning
obscures
the scent of the vines
of your flesh and blood

At noon I watch
your naked body in the shade
that moves

Under moon's cover
and the sound of the reeds
I will force myself to wait
to be alone with you

what have you done?

under moon's cover
and the sound of the reeds
we burned our vessels
bare in battle

and then?

dissipated moon
silent reeds
we slept
solitudes exhausted
we slept

Who compares
your cry
and the cry of the nubile bird catcher

Tonight you appear vast

carousel of horses
on the strings of the lute

woman of pains

heavy night
of ramparts of clay

will it be for blood

the chord would cease
tonight

drought has burned everything

beasts
and the hearts of men

in your eyes

carousel of horses
on the strings of the lute

on your life

the shadow of your lashes
would end thirst

captive

let's remain here    woman of grief
here is a home

lasting in time

of white stone
and sepulture

The sky
by fibers
was taken in the sands

the wind shifted this morning
pushed away the rain
farther than sight

but the wind does not erase
the trace of the flight
of open birds

the sky
is like our guts

I sense
I watch for your waking
same as that of the moon

your hands open
I tell you

I made a comb for your hair
and I hollowed the black stone
to find its heart
and the shadow for your eyes

when we reach
sight of the olive trees
hung to the earth
of changing ochre

when we reach
sight of the ramparts
I will take the knife and the rifle
and the slowness of the seasons

in my gut
a reminiscent dream
in my hands
the smell of the beasts
the burning bark
down below
the nocturnal sound of reeds
in my body

the patience of the night
and something in your eyes
darkens
darkens

too long
this time of clay
branded with rumors and crushed senses

I want to die
and capture your look
passing

like birds leaving
in the slowness of the sky

Fatma dreams

wells
punctuate thirst

she speaks

her song is soft
like the sand
under my steps

she invokes

the power of scorpions
mortal passion

Oblique guitar
Andalusian viola
smothered
do you think me foreign
to death nearing

the days
buried
in your eyes
lashes
ritual

do you see
the line of the wind
white sepulture
no end
to sand

attentive
the sailor eye
withering opacity

liquid nacre
vision of the world

the ocean wind
passes
dying heart
work of silence
and resentment

the saffron sky and you
offered appearances
inverted earth
between the dream
and extreme solitude

bird of lava
in sudden white sky
watery eye
of the air
of time

making of silence
the matter
of rain

is it your voice
that I hear

gone
desert essences
naked
between the somber hour
and the ocean

∽

On iron bridges of air
despairing of the wind
why?

I set icy rules
for my burning body
and then

maybe the sky buried

fire calcifies
the inventory
your red mouth
and your mystical eyes of antimony

maybe the sky

constructing your logical body
forgetting    that is necessary
lagoon colors
red Orient and lugubrious moments

awaiting

each one of us dies
in precise circumstances

life is incised
each one of us dies

I would have liked    internal echoes
again to touch
the fertile signs

the weariness of time

the path of the stars
between your lashes

what lyricism
what losses of time

oceans
derived from silence

∾

will you wait for me if I tarry?

birds     external echoes
and I find the plot of the journey

hallow sky and white sand

escaping from one moment
to the next death surely coming
who poisonous comes

what lyricism
this silence          delectable

what can I tell you in words?

I must renounce you mud of light
I must open roads of stone and of reversed sky
I must open the veins of a somber horse
to the dance enclosed in a ray of the moon
I must do more than brush the dawn elongated in the blue
I must die from your beauty and its negation

The day will disintegrate in its diaphanous filth

I will put my hand on your soul
I will put light in your body
like a lamp

I will caress the troughs of your dreams
like God caresses Harlem
to appease her

you will be the mortal jasmine that I have
in total patience invented

Between death and me
there is a bond of red silk
a promise of jubilation

pale eyelids
boats and thresholds of the verse
black lashes heavy and straight

flight eternally delayed
moon in retrograde
place of love in silence

Passage of sounds far away
a voyage ringed with rust and blood

I could refuse the absolute games of dusk
evidence of the unimaginable

I could refuse to enchant rotten tomorrows

but   light of betrayal
I devise the silence
of this world
drop by drop
I drain the poison

∞

I am the mud of the potter dead for centuries
I am sacrificial bulls overhanging the sea
I am studded with the turquoise with pestilence
dreamer in the night abstracted from any imaginary essence

I am the hot entrails of a city opened
bent this night and every night on destruction
I am hours of happiness in the houses of others
I am the undergrowth of stars a man without utility

I am the assassin in a blue hesitation
I am the lover of death
I am the painter of my eyes

∽

Prey dreamed by the bitter lover
with what are we to live?

on your white skin
like a shadow

like the trace of bird
a refined tattoo

∽

I left
but I was scorched by your tepid fire

your life
space of tepid fire passing through me

∽

Eyelids lowered
partial worlds
quiet

*Wild Donkey and Solitudes*

We had a long conversation
with the wild donkey
one on one

paranoia of evening
and paranoia of morning
are delicate flowers

A dream
divided in two

destinies meet
like animals

I saw the corpse of the plum tree
of the camel his splattered guts
the soiled tears of the child
the sniffle of orphan light

I abandoned the pursuit of art
to sleep for eternity
under the fevered feet of my children

Reflecting from space
all the illusions

the acrid light
the emptiness and the stare

cats on rubble
blue on the beach

a whirling seagull
circles a jug of rust

a swimmer indulges
in magic

he is painting on his skin
a motif in black ink

The slave was sucking
a golden sweet
in Yemen

her mouth closed
around the space
of night

it was a sculpture
flesh of lips of chill
of bronze

because the stray master
goes astray when he
dances

Noon
female ocelot
love is a cold shadow

∽

Fart of the sublime orca
blue oceans heaved
from Fez to Arabia
dances and words
ropes and clouds

golden visions of the sailor in the city
three tears of orchid
it's a poem in memory of a luncheon
with Fatma Leila and Jean Genet

༄

The order comes from afar

I ignore the sweetness
that follows

hordes
of limpid horses
graze my lying body

it's a blue herb
that vanquishes me with its vague folds

dead
between the lashes

obscure lines
tracing the absence

this thing
that gently glows

◌

Gentle
line
of sleepiness

white field
where horses of grief scatter me

I breathe you
and I die

I am pinto
gelding of steppes
the winged passage in the burning cities

I will whinny tomorrow with normal madness
in the fluid morning
for no reason

I am a note of music
horse without destiny

the man is dead before electrifying
his mandolin

before going back on his steps
he is dead under the moon
of calendars

the mane of wind was erased

it will take thorough organization

for the organization of the funeral

or a miracle

a ranch in Andalusia
for man-pinto

God

silence

stop and end

boredom

∞

Two thousand moons dissolve
sluggish and slow
the obscure duty to harmonize
tambourines flames and blood
and guitars of the festivities

bewitching people
nauseated

fever on my leash
I caress the palms
and slow surfaces
I smoke blue vision

reason worsens
heart wounded

I    so rare
I don't even know how to make
papers light    black powder
evil    brutal ideas
 and leave

∽

In the crash of silence preceding death
I amaze myself that a slim idea like
a piece of paper
slipped
a confusing idea of light under the door

Alicante the summer like décor

*Poems of Immobile Love*

∽

We find nothing in the depths of the days

waters between stones
stones between skies

only
the slowness

of death we give ourselves

Scattering of stars
animal wounds

first there is the sacrifice

and then the red sky running
in a narrow passage

∽

The rumor I hear is the cry of a throat of sand
the sense is lost in the distances bleached from time
he said   bury my heart in the heart of my country
he begs for the millennial lethargy of silt
from the heart of the earth emerge cotton flowers
transparent spheres still suffering from birth
supine     sweat     splinters in the heart     betrayals
lyric preparation obscurities of song
cities of metal ringed with jazz of blood

to be the first     flesh open
to name oneself     to be the fire of a voice
perfumed openings     illusions of arches   of passages
fountains and solitude     tar   vertigo
the malediction to be a frontier
energy     pure     pain
emerald travail left in the ebb of doom

the rumor I hear is a dying echo
scratches of silence     scattered notes of mandolin
Andalusian sky over the land of Palestine

bodies bent before submitting
obscure horses browse the horizon
hooves of nacre     leaden chests
terrible nights of moons of blood
in lazy pastures serene animals molder

∽

Pure reality like the idea of a blade
honey of fading shadow
infinite grief
your pain is mine
vulgar country
at the somber pinks of the hour
that precedes the mineral sadness
vague divisions
by the subtle flags
of errant bodies
under the moldering skies
there's the flutter of palms
polished by time
there's a prerequisite look


love is pursued
like  transparence

Carriers of water
shoulders restrained to the order of the world
bitterness and silt

carriers of fire
splinters in the body of silence
the fall of Granada was
an explosion of flavors

carriers of destiny
tell the powdery butterflies of memory
how does the Orient finish
how does it begin

*A la Señora F.B.*


Disjointed from love
its taste
mixes fruit and metal

in the clear reflection of night
I have the head of a Turk

and I think tenderly
tenderly?

of a poet and a painter
Andalusian

*Poem for my little girl who dances naked on the solid table where I write*

Blade of bird
disentangles lines of sadness
imaginary lines

for him who travels
there is no sadness

there are blades in the heart
and traces in the sky
that are birds

*Vision of the Return of Khadija to Opium*

∽

You run on the plains of death without fearing any obstacle
black plough soft scents like traces of love on the skin of
the beloved you gallop fluid without advancing a step
conscience inundated with the smoke of blue herbs you
escape from fear and enchantment brushing crimson shores
and traps of light languages of love and the distress of
meaning and the gold of the dagger thrusts in the burst
of the cry and the sob


you stop breath weak lost body from you to yourself and in
the virgin space of golden death by the hourly borders of
the ultimate transparence you recognize in her the familiar
dead the beloved of unhappiness so urgent to lament her
her dead body laid softly returning gravely to love her dead
eye of the sun caught in the pain of her dying body on the
shore of the untouchable self


you are no more the sensitive prisoner rolling in the flight
the rust the hair the bleached static of your body captive
memory stopped in the silence of midday perfumes the odor

of liberty white opacity that expands it's the death of you
that touches me and brushes me with your fingers and pulls
me toward your body of sadness neglecting

you silence me to myself injured body by chance blind
tracing common aches tears births like light in the heart of
the accident of the fatal rhythm of dazzling hooves gold
fire error of the hand on the neck odor too ripe of the mane
sweaty body of the lover the runaway frightened by the
violence of the brassy hordes of chance

you sink the arm and the shoulder when lingers the regard
of the disappointed lover too soft the skin of her hand on
your body useless supplication of silence you sink an ancient
light you're dying from feeling all the pain of the simulacra
of the sleeping in the design of the lamp in your eye at night

you don't have the strength the desire you no longer
recognize your actions and your lovers withdraw one after
the other behind a drape thick red like blood you no longer
recognize your country your people the servants of your
fantasy stay clear and you remain the only captive of the
absolute sadness of death

you knew the blue and the ochre unspoken and offered your veins to silence you confused numbers and people in the joy you confronted the deadline by sliding your language in hers you transformed yourself into seed of shadow in more than a memory you fractured the luminous trouble into essential stones lost in the confusion of a stony atmosphere you slept in the cruelty of absence

you are stopping me once again from coming to you even though you lightly touch me you rouse me lover extinguished dark forever you keep me at a distance for yourself useless for the hours for the fatal passengers of the immobile wreck useless you protect me with your gaze dead fixed dark excessive you welcome me with the extreme languor of your only certitude

you don't have any love any doubt any sensation for the servitude of those whom love devours you move among the fragile emerald lozenges of Hannibal's dusk you push your metal in the living flesh of those who hold onto the edge of another time fastening their bodies of ancient pain of infertile life prisoners erased from their fragile destiny who await you who go nowhere who take no path devoured by love innocent aching until the sudden instant of your encounter

you designate from afar traces of slavery of roads dusty
with a false light that falls from a pale sky of barbarity you
awake and appoint eternal journeys smoldering odors of the
voyage of the unbelievers you play with their lucidity until
the atrocious vomiting of ultimate truths you assassinate
those who invoke another name another gesture of iron in
the earth and in the loam you turn around and you fall sleep
while the lover watches exhausts the precious light of a lying
eye dead from imperious sun


you incise the painful signs of survivals in the atrocity of the
trials of the race in the parched flesh and the bitter core in
the most impoverished symbols of the enigma of the body
that a blade's distance kills reflection of silver metal and
bitter flame between the doomed bodies


you separate me from those who I love from the world
from matutinal flights of blue birds in a sky of pale water
you bring me back to the sad order of days tearing rough
silk wearied by so many hands sticky in the filth of morning
earths the mist escapes like the dream that flees from us
crepuscular smokers broken bits of the cortège of useless
dreamers

you have no other empire than our bodies kneaded with lies than our lives separated by the knife of misfortune and doom than our will limed in the bad sleep of malediction slow malediction for the derisory tribe no more pity for you no more misery in the look when they see you chasing the shadows of the past oscillating like the memory of a white mule at noon lost among the rocks

you touch me with your scent you overcome me with the same slight perpetual feeling autumnal irrationality of my body that the pain of crippled loves imprison no honeyed light and space no tranquil domain of offered transparencies you tear off clothes of gold and pardon of courtesans fragile inlay of amber perspiration that pearls on your skin on mine you leave your scent you yield because the chronology of love is again absurd

you rip the veil of death perfumed by the softness of your shoulder time goes by in the clasped gardens of stone time tears courts of eroded turquoise staircases of blanched threatened jasmine time goes by we divine the port but no departure and in my heart no freedom

you are absent in the darkness of time in pale fractures
of smoldering houses for the runaway you leave only the
gathering of odors of ashed landscape let him walk let him
return to the sad houses of illusion let him cross the black
and the white let him smolder let him be hurt let him
surrender himself to the sands of migrating sands and
wind that halt neither will nor respiration


you pass in the distance of the plains of death
unaccomplished body of obscure ardor you cross my
conscience and the approach of your body burns me fan
the weakened light you yourself free to cross body and
soul free to burn the essences far and soft of the miserable
dream pass in the distance you who shares me you that the
griefs embellish and now stumble because I want you

AMIN KHAN was born in Algiers during the Algerian War of Independence in 1956. He grew up in a revolutionary family, writing poetry, and nurturing interests in philosophy and politics. Studies at the University of Algiers, the University of Oxford and the *Insitut d'Études Politiques* in Paris followed. As a diplomat and international civil servant, he held positions at the United Nations (New York), The World Bank (Washington, D.C.) and UNESCO in Paris, where he now lives with his family. His books include *Les Mains de Fatma* (Sned 1982) and *Archipel Cobalt* (MLD 2010), as well as the forthcoming *Arabian blues* (MLD 2012).